All About Boats

Consultant:
Adria F. Klein, PhD
California State University, San Bernardino

CAPSTONE PRESS
a capstone imprint

Wonder Readers are published by Capstone Press,
1710 Roe Crest Drive, North Mankato, Minnesota 56003.
www.capstonepub.com

Books published by Capstone Press are manufactured with paper
containing at least 10 percent post-consumer waste.

Library of Congress Cataloging-in-Publication Data
Lindeen, Mary.
  All about boats / Mary Lindeen. — 1st ed.
    p. cm. — (Wonder readers)
  ISBN 978-1-4296-7906-0 (paperback)
  ISBN 978-1-4296-8639-6 (library binding)
  1. Boats and boating—Juvenile literature. 2. Ships—Juvenile literature. I. Title.
  VM150.L493 2012
  623.82—dc23   696 5076   2011021996

Summary: Simple text and color photos present boat history, working boats, and recreational boats.

Note to Parents and Teachers

The Wonder Readers: Social Studies series supports national social studies
standards. These titles use text structures that support early readers, specifically
with a close photo/text match and glossary. Each book is perfectly leveled to
support the reader at the right reading level, and the topics are of high interest.
Early readers will gain success when they are presented with a book that is of
interest to them and is written at the appropriate level.

Printed in the United States of America in North Mankato, Minnesota.
102011   006405CGS12

Table of Contents

Early Boats

Boats have been around almost as long as people have. Humans learned what many animals already knew. Traveling on water is a quick way to get from one place to another. Sometimes it's the only way!

Early boats were built from logs, tree bark, and animal skins. Paddles helped to move and steer the boats. **Canoes** were some of the earliest kinds of boats.

Builders began making larger boats.
Large boats are called ships. Early
ships moved using wind power.
Wind pushed against the cloth sails,
and that pushed the ships through
the water.

Riverboats carried people and supplies up and down rivers. The boats were powered by steam engines that turned the big paddle wheels.

Working Boats

This big **barge** is getting help from a small but powerful tugboat. The tugboat is pulling the barge to help steer it into the harbor. The tugboat captain has to watch both boats carefully to guide them to the right spot.

Fireboats are like fire trucks on water. They put out fires on ships or in buildings that are near the water. Sometimes fireboats are the only way to fight those fires. They use pumps on board to spray sea, lake, or river water on the flames.

This boat works in water that is so cold it freezes over. The **icebreaker** breaks through thick ice to make a path for other boats. It is like a snowplow on water.

A **ferry** takes people and their vehicles from one landing to another. People drive onto the boat and park. They can get out and enjoy the view during the ride. When they reach their destination, they just drive off the boat and away they go!

Fun Boats

Huge **cruise ships** take people from one ocean port to another. It is like taking a vacation on a floating hotel. Cruise ships have restaurants, movie theaters, and swimming pools on board.

A sailboat uses wind power to move across the water. These sailboats are in a race. Each team is trying to sail as fast as it can to be the first to finish the course.

Speedboats use powerful motors to move fast across the water. They can pull people on water skis or wakeboards. The skier holds on to a rope attached to the back of the boat and zips across the water.

A **hydroplane** skims just above the surface of the water. This one is a racing boat. It can go as fast as 200 miles (320 kilometers) per hour! Hydroplane races are exciting to watch.

Boats in the Future

This boat travels underwater. It can go all the way down to the bottom of the ocean. Scientists inside use robotic tools on the outside of the boat to study the ocean floor.

This is a boat that was built for making movies underwater. There are lights and cameras on board. Just imagine the boats that will be floating around in the future. Maybe you will be lucky enough to ride on one!

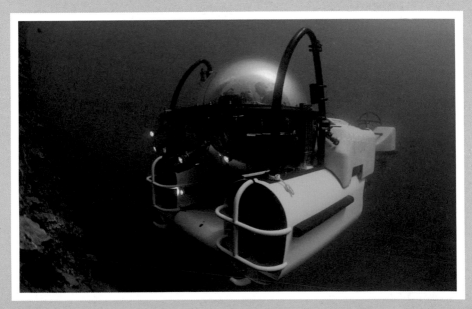

Glossary

barge   a long boat with a flat bottom, used for hauling cargo

canoe   a light, narrow boat that moves by paddling

cruise ship   a large boat that takes people on vacations

ferry   a boat that regularly carries people and cars across the water

fireboat   a boat that puts out fires on the water

hydroplane   a fast boat that moves just above the surface of the water

icebreaker   a boat built to break up ocean ice so that ships can pass

Now Try This!

Write the name of each kind of boat from the book on a note card. Then sort the boats into groups based on the chapter headings in the book (early boats, working boats, fun boats, boats in the future) Think of a way to group the boats into three groups. Next think of a way to group the boats into two groups. Which task was easier? Which was more difficult? Why do you think so?

Internet Sites

FactHound offers a safe, fun way to find Internet sites related to this book. All of the sites on FactHound have been researched by our staff.

Here's all you do:

Visit *www.facthound.com*

Type in this code: 9781429686396

Super-cool stuff!

Check out projects, games and lots more at
www.capstonekids.com

Index

Editorial Credits

Maryellen Gregoire, project director; Mary Lindeen, consulting editor; Gene Bentdahl, designer; Sarah Schuette, editor; Wanda Winch, media researcher; Laura Manthe, production specialist

Photo Credits

Corbis: Jeffrey Rotman, 17; Shutterstock: 1971yes, 6, Anne Kitzman, 7, Antonio Abrignani, 4, Darren Baker, 13, Darren Brode, 15, Jeff Banke, 9, Joy Prescott, 8, Luigi Nifosi, 1, Maria Dryfhout, 5, Milos Jaric, 11, Noel Powell, Schaumburg, 12, Ramunas Bruzas, cover, tubuceo, 16, VikOl, 10, wheatley, 14

Word Count: **491**   Guided Reading Level: **K**   Early Intervention Level: **18**